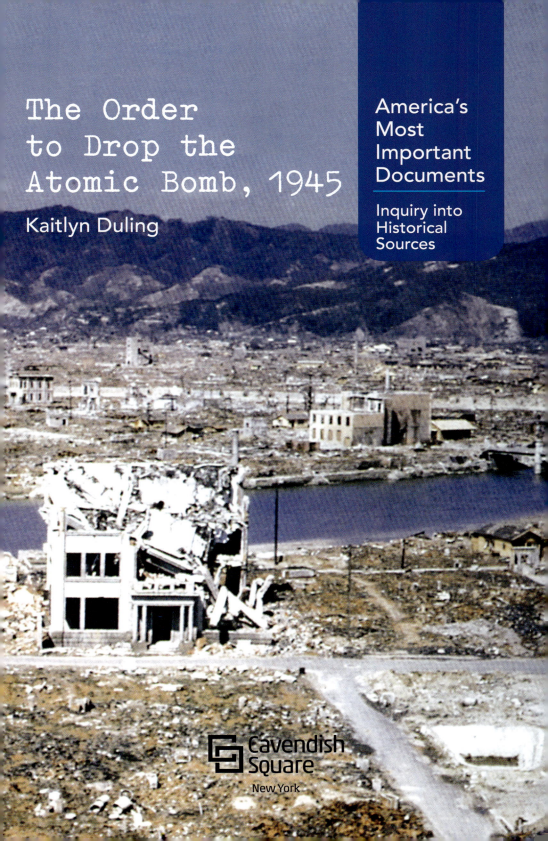

The Order to Drop the Atomic Bomb, 1945

Kaitlyn Duling

America's Most Important Documents

Inquiry into Historical Sources

Cavendish Square
New York

Published in 2019 by Cavendish Square Publishing, LLC
243 5th Avenue, Suite 136, New York, NY 10016

Copyright © 2019 by Cavendish Square Publishing, LLC

First Edition

No part of this publication may be reproduced, stored in a retrieval system, or transmitted in any form or by any means—electronic, mechanical, photocopying, recording, or otherwise—without the prior permission of the copyright owner. Request for permission should be addressed to Permissions, Cavendish Square Publishing, 243 5th Avenue, Suite 136, New York, NY 10016. Tel (877) 980-4450; fax (877) 980-4454.

Website: cavendishsq.com

This publication represents the opinions and views of the author based on his or her personal experience, knowledge, and research. The information in this book serves as a general guide only. The author and publisher have used their best efforts in preparing this book and disclaim liability rising directly or indirectly from the use and application of this book.

All websites were available and accurate when this book was sent to press.

Cataloging-in-Publication Data

Names: Duling, Kaitlyn.
Title: The order to drop the atomic bomb, 1945 / Kaitlyn Duling.
Description: New York : Cavendish Square, 2019. | Series: America's most important documents: inquiry into historical sources | Includes glossary and index.
Identifiers: ISBN 9781502636218 (pbk.) | ISBN 9781502636195 (library bound) | ISBN 9781502636201 (ebook)
Subjects: LCSH: Atomic bomb--Juvenile literature. | World War, 1939-1945--Campaigns--Japan--Juvenile literature. | Hiroshima-shi (Japan)--History--Bombardment, 1945--Juvenile literature.
Classification: LCC D767.25.H6 D85 2019 | DDC 940.54'252--dc23

Editorial Director: David McNamara
Editor: Kristen Susienka
Copy Editor: Alex Tessman
Associate Art Director: Amy Greenan
Designer: Joe Parenteau
Production Coordinator: Karol Szymczuk
Photo Research: J8 Media

The photographs in this book are used by permission and through the courtesy of: Cover: Prisma by Dukas Presseagentur GmbH/Alamy Stock Photo; p. 4 PhotoQuest/Getty Images; p. 7, 14 Bettmann/Getty Images; p. 9 ShadeDesign/Shutterstock.com; p. 12 Hulton Archive/Getty Images; p. 16 MyLoupe/UIG/Getty Images; p. 17, 18 Corbis/Getty Images; p. 21 Library of Congress/Corbis/Getty Images; p. 22 Hulton-Deutsch Collection/Corbis/Getty Images; p. 26 509th Operations Group/Wikimedia Commons/File:Atomic cloud over Hiroshima (from Matsuyama).jpg/Public Domain; p. 27, 28 Universal History Archive/UIG/Getty Images; p. 31 Paul Popper/Popperfoto/Getty Images; p. 33 Pavalena/Shutterstock.com; p. 35 Dan Thornberg/Shutterstock.com; p. 37 George Rinhart/Corbis/Getty Images; p. 39, 47 Popperfoto/Getty Images; p. 41 Thomas D. Mcavoy/The LIFE Picture Collection/Getty Images; p. 42 Andrew Biraj/AFP/Getty Images; p. 45 Rolls Press/Popperfoto/Getty Images; p. 48 Underwood Archives/Getty Images; p. 50 Gerasimov Foto 174/Shutterstock.com; p. 52 STR/AFP/Getty Images.

Printed in the United States of America

Contents

1 Building the Bomb 5

2 A Decision Is Made 23

3 Leaving a Legacy 43

   Glossary. 54

   Further Information 57

   Bibliography. 59

   Index 62

   About the Author 64

Chapter One

Building the Bomb

Can you imagine a time before atomic weapons? An era in which countries did not and could not threaten one another with total, complete destruction? A time before "weapons of mass destruction," the Cold War, or nuclear missile tests? For most of our planet's history, people were unable to destroy our world on such cataclysmic levels. In fact, until the mid-1930s, atomic weapons were left up to science-fiction novels and scientists with big imaginations. Wars were fought and won using guns, cannons, submarines, and conventional bombs that could blow up a building, maybe even a few buildings at once, but not an entire town. Not a whole city, miles wide. Not an entire small island. Not like that.

Opposite: The atomic bomb Little Boy would be dropped onto the Japanese city of Hiroshima in August 1945.

World War II

A weapon like the atomic bomb might have been imagined during peacetime, but it took a state of war, a perceived threat, to prompt the development and creation of such a deadly weapon. World War II began in earnest on September 1, 1939, with Germany's invasion of Poland. At the time, Germany was ruled by a Nazi dictator named Adolf Hitler. The Nazis were members of the National Socialist German Workers' Party, a political group that hated those who appeared to be different from them, specifically people of Jewish descent. Hitler wanted to rule Europe, beginning with Poland. He had dreams of ruling the world and wouldn't let anyone stand in his way. To try to stop the Nazi advance, France and Britain both declared war on Germany on September 3. At this point, it was no longer a simple power struggle between two countries, or even two ideologies. From that moment on, the war would heat up, bubble and ooze its way across Europe, North Africa, and the Middle East, though these early stages centered on the tumultuous European landscape.

Soon, Hitler partnered with Italy's dictator, Benito Mussolini, and they jointly pursued their goals of acquiring more land. A year later, the overall territory of the war expanded when Germany and Italy came together with Japan, a country that longed to be the dominant power in Asia. These three countries would come to be known as the Axis powers. As 1940 crept along, the Japanese captured territory in Asia that was previously held by Britain. In the United States, President Franklin Roosevelt looked to the West and the East, but didn't want to dive headfirst into another war, despite a desire to support Britain. World War I had ended in 1918, just over twenty years prior. It would take a serious turn of events to spur the United States into another conflict overseas.

Adolf Hitler used rousing speeches and scare tactics to convince German citizens to side with his Nazi Party.

Pearl Harbor

It wouldn't be many months, however, until an event occurred that would set the war on a crash course, hurtling toward the creation of the world's deadliest weapon. On December 7, 1941, Pearl Harbor, one of America's main naval bases, on the Hawaiian island of Oahu, was destroyed in a surprise attack by Japanese aircraft. The attack was sudden, unexpected, and deadly. Over 2,500 American sailors lost their lives. Ships and planes were destroyed. To the United States, this appeared to be a declaration of war. The very next day, the United States and Britain declared war on Japan. Then the Axis powers came to the aid of Japan and, on December 11, declared war on the United States. Eventually, the war's structure would be split between the Axis powers and the Allied powers: Great Britain, the United States, China, and the Soviet Union. The stage was set for a years-long power struggle that could accurately hold the name "world war."

Can We Split the Atom?

Long before the attack on Pearl Harbor, the United States was already considering new, more powerful weapons that could be used if the country entered the war. In fact, the secrets behind the atomic bomb were conceived long before World War I and World War II.

Some elements, like uranium and plutonium, emit energetic waves or particles. This is called radiation. The idea of radioactivity (or radioactive decay) was first discovered in 1898 by a woman named Marie Curie. She was a French chemist. These energetic waves not only make a weapon explode with extreme force, but they also linger. After a reaction occurs (like a nuclear bomb explosion), radiation settles into the atmosphere, as well as into the ground and into the bodies of people. Radioactive particles can remain in the highest parts of our atmosphere for years following an explosion.

A few years later, in 1911, a British physicist named Ernest Rutherford built on Curie's discovery, completing his own

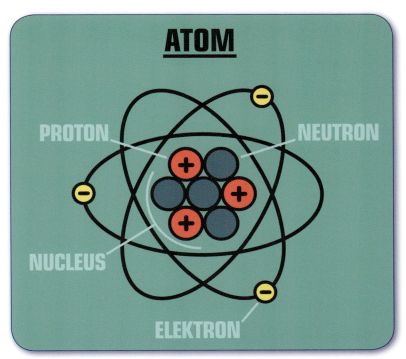

Inside an atom's nucleus you can find protons and neutrons. Electron particles are in motion outside the nucleus.

research into the nearly limitless energy that could be found at the heart of every atom. Atoms are the minuscule particles that make up our world. They cannot be seen with the naked eye. Each atom has a nucleus at its center, with charged particles moving furiously around it. If these forces could somehow be released, the potential for energy would be immense!

From the turn of the twentieth century into the 1930s, scientists in England, Germany, and other European countries would continue with molecular research that would broaden our understanding of atoms, their parts, and what could happen when atoms of different elements collide. In 1939, a discovery was made that would put the world on a more direct course to the atomic bomb. Scientists Otto Hahn, Fritz Strassmann, and Lise Meitner discovered the process of nuclear fission. In its most basic form, nuclear fission occurs when the middle (nucleus) of a heavy atomic atom is divided into multiple parts. This division creates massive amounts of energy, much more so than in a chemical reaction. If you stacked a pile of TNT explosives ten stories high, it would be almost as explosive as a tiny piece of uranium that was about to go through nuclear fission. This was the process that gave these scientists a glimpse of what could happen if these elements were harnessed for use in weapons. That glimpse was not a positive one.

    The key to making a powerful weapon that utilized nuclear fission was to take advantage of the domino effect. Picture a line of dominos set up on the floor. When you knock over the first domino, all the rest fall down, one by one. Nuclear reactions happen the same way, as atoms split, creating more and more energy. One atom splits in two, and then those two split, creating four, and then those four split, and the pattern continues. All along, greater amounts of energy are being released. This is also called a chain reaction. A Hungarian scientist named Leo Szilard played a central role in the discovery of nuclear chain reactions, and was one of the first to truly devise how an atomic bomb might work. Nuclear chain reactions would eventually be used to build nuclear power plants that could generate electricity, powering some of the world's largest cities. But in the midst of World War II, electricity generation was not on the minds of European scientists like Szilard. The potential for a new kind of bomb was all they could see.

During this time of discovery, the greater scientific community, particularly physicists, grew deeply concerned about the prospect of atomic weapons. Szilard had emigrated from Hungary to live in the United States, and he wrote many letters to the US government, warning them that the Nazis could easily harness the research to create their own atomic weapon. But the US government wasn't listening. In the summer of 1939, just as Hitler was coming to power and getting ready to invade Poland, a group of physicists joined together to write a letter to President Roosevelt. They wanted to warn the president about the harm that could come from Germany developing a uranium-based weapon before the United States did. Leo Szilard, Eugene Wigner, and Edward Teller took their concerns—and their letter—to Albert Einstein, a world-renowned physicist, Nobel Prize winner, and creator of the theory of relativity. Much nuclear research had been based off of Einstein's theory, directly implicating him in the work. Einstein was also very well known internationally, and had a relationship with the Roosevelt family. Einstein signed the letter.

Though the letter was signed in August, it didn't reach President Roosevelt until October 11, 1939. The outbreak of the war had significantly slowed the letter's progress to the president's desk. It was delivered by Alexander Sachs, one of Roosevelt's trusted and longtime advisors. The letter both informed the president of the science and warned him of the dangers at hand:

> *In the course of the last four months it has been made probable ... to set up a nuclear chain reaction in a large mass of uranium, by which vast amounts*

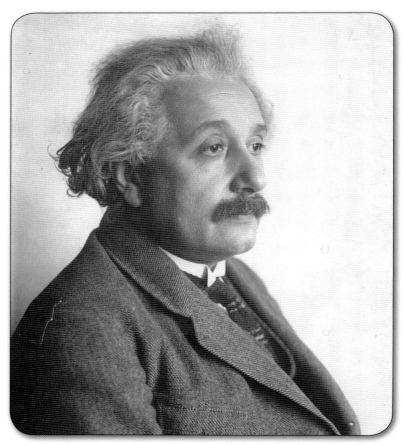

Albert Einstein, a world-renowned physicist, was drawn into early conversations surrounding nuclear fission and the possibility of a bomb.

> *of power and large quantities of new radium-like elements would be generated ... This new phenomenon would also lead to the construction of bombs ... a single bomb of this type, carried by boat and exploded in a port, might very well destroy the whole port together with some of the surrounding territory.*

After reading the letter, Roosevelt became convinced that nuclear fission was important, but he was not swayed by its urgency. As presidents often do when new information is brought to their attention, he created an advisory committee to study the matter. However, the events of December 7, 1941, would bring the idea back into focus. As the United States entered the war, the time to actively pursue the creation of an atomic weapon was suddenly there. The United States government secretly and quietly decided that it needed to be the first country to harness the years of nuclear research into the creation of an atomic bomb.

The Manhattan Project

By 1942, the president had decided to move the project out of committee and into active development. He also decided to finally put government funding behind the efforts, a key component if a bomb would ever be created. In the spring of that year, scientists were hard at work in labs across the country, working to create enough fissionable material to make a bomb. The largest and most notable labs were located at Columbia University in New York City, the University of Chicago, and the University of California, Berkeley. From coast to coast and in the Midwest, researchers worked around the clock. The first headquarters of the project was in New York City, at the Manhattan Engineering District. This is why the project came to be known as the Manhattan Project.

Because the efforts were so urgent, militaristic, large, and far-reaching, the Manhattan Project was placed under the purview of the US Army, and Leslie Groves, an army officer, was chosen as director. This was a pivot from where

The Los Alamos Scientific Laboratory was discreetly situated in the New Mexican desert.

the knowledge had originally centered itself, with European physicists, many of whom were Jewish scientists who had fled Germany and its occupied territories. With Groves at the helm, the project became extremely physical. Huge tracts of land were purchased at different sites across the country, and secret cities were built in order to house the tens of thousands of workers that would be needed for the effort. While he was traveling in California, General Groves met J. Robert Oppenheimer, an ambitious physicist. He would take a lead role in the research and eventual creation of the bomb.

The project's central lab was located on a remote property in New Mexico that used to be a wilderness school for boys. It would come to be known as Los Alamos. The site was isolated in order to give scientists a space for the exchange of ideas. Oppenheimer became the research director for the site. Rows and rows of cheap houses were constructed within the high, barbed-wire fence that surrounded the Los Alamos property. Many of the world's greatest scientists moved to Los Alamos to work on the project, along with workers who would physically build the components for the atomic bomb.

Two Bombs

Eventually, the scientists at Los Alamos would produce two different types of atomic bombs. The first was called Little Boy. It functioned like a gun—a chunk of uranium was shot down the barrel of the bomb, colliding with another piece of uranium, starting the chain reaction that would, theoretically, cause a massive explosion.

The second bomb was called Fat Man. This bomb contained a sphere of plutonium that was then covered with TNT explosives. When detonated, the TNT would compress the plutonium into a dense mass, which would then start its own chain reaction. This is called an implosion, because things inside are

And Furthermore

The US government perceived its efforts to build the bomb as part of a greater "race" for atomic weapons. Leaders and researchers worried that other countries would develop the technology—and possibly use it—before the United States. To ensure that America would win, some $2 billion were poured into the Manhattan Project. More than forty thousand people were employed in some facet of the project. For a secret initiative, the atom bomb project was extremely well resourced.

These replicas of Little Boy (*left*) and Fat Man (*right*) show their size relative to each other.

being squeezed together. In the spring of 1945, designs for both bombs were finished and approved.

Trinity Test

Meanwhile, World War II was plodding on. The United States was actively bombing Japan using air raids, conventional explosives dropped from airplanes. Tens of thousands of Japanese civilians were killed in each air raid, yet the United States continued to put on the pressure. Japan would not back down. The United States might still need to utilize their atomic bomb, and before they used it in battle, they had to see if all of the research had come together to create something that worked. Oppenheimer scheduled a test of Fat Man for the

The successful Trinity test was captured in this photograph on July 16, 1945.

summer of 1945. He was nearly certain that Little Boy would be a success, but he wanted to put the implosion bomb to the test. It would be called the Trinity test, and it was top secret. At this point, American citizens, most government officials, and even the vice president were all unaware of the research and development of the atomic bombs. While planning for Trinity, the team came up with press releases that would go out on the day of the test, owing the huge explosion to an accident at a weapons factory.

As everyone readied for the Trinity test, building a tall steel tower from which to drop the bomb and plotting out safe distances from which to watch, two events radically changed the atomic outlook. On April 12, 1945, President Roosevelt died from a brain hemorrhage. Suddenly, Harry S. Truman became the US president charged with commanding the military and the atomic bomb project, though nearly every aspect of the Manhattan Project had been kept a secret from him as vice

In 1945, city blocks were completely leveled during summer firebomb raids in Tokyo, Japan.

> ### And Furthermore
>
> After the attack on Pearl Harbor, President Roosevelt ordered that Japanese Americans be relocated to camps called internment camps. The president feared Japanese Americans might be spies for the enemy. About 115,000 people were incarcerated at the camps. Even those with minimal Japanese heritage were sent. This was an unjust treatment of a group of people and apologies have been made in the decades since.

president. One month later, on May 8, 1945, Germany surrendered. The war in Europe had come to an end, and Hitler was dead. The bomb would not be needed in the fight with Germany or with Italy, as Mussolini had surrendered in 1943. It was up to President Truman to look toward Japan and decide if an atomic weapon was needed in order to close out World War II in its final theater.

As crews in New Mexico loaded up the steel tower for the Trinity test, the Japanese continued to fight, despite American blockades of food and supplies and deadly fire bombings. Fire bombs were meant to set cities ablaze. During one six-hour period of fire bombing, one hundred thousand people lost their lives, more loss than in any equivalent time period in history. Additionally, thousands of American soldiers continued to lose their lives, while many prisoners of war were subjected to extremely harsh conditions from the Japanese military. As the days ticked by, President Truman continuously surveyed the situation, waiting on a call from General Groves to hear if the test had worked.

At 5:29 a.m. on July 16, 1945, in the middle of the New Mexican desert, the detonation occurred. Slowly, yet suddenly,

The Final Push: An Offer to Surrender

By July 1945, it was time for the war with Japan to end. On July 26, the United States, Soviet Union, and Great Britain came together to issue a demand for Japanese surrender. On that day, the parts for the two new bombs were flown to a US air base on the Pacific island of Tinian. The call for surrender was known as the Potsdam Declaration, and it was a strongly worded document. However, Japan did not surrender.

About ten days later, the United States decided to drop the bomb. August 6, 1945, became a day that would forever be marked in history: the dropping of the first atomic bomb.

a gigantic orb of fire and light grew bulbous in the night sky, its heat and light expanding outward. As J. Robert Oppenheimer watched his years of research and development explode into the sky before him, he later said that his mind went to the Bhagavad Gita, a Hindu scripture. Years later, recalling the moment, he said, "A few people laughed, a few people cried, most people were silent. I remembered the line … 'Now I am become death, the destroyer of worlds.' I suppose we all thought that, one way or another."

The test had been a success. It revealed the incredible power of what the team had created—explosion, destruction, intense heat and light. Immediately following the test, General Groves and Oppenheimer began working on a report for President Truman and Secretary of War Henry Lewis Stimson. That very day, Truman had arrived at the Potsdam Conference, a meeting of the Allies to discuss the war with Japan. Stimson received a telegram from his special assistant on atomic issues, George L. Harrison:

Henry Lewis Stimson worked closely with President Truman leading up to the dropping of the atomic bomb.

> *Operated on this morning. Diagnosis not yet complete but results seem satisfactory and already exceed expectations. Local press release necessary as interest extends great distance. Dr. Groves pleased. He returns tomorrow. I will keep you posted.*

He related the coded telegram to President Truman. The test had been successful. The United States had won the race to create an atomic weapon. Now, Truman would have to decide when, where—and if—this deadly, destructive bomb would be dropped.

Chapter Two

A Decision Is Made

The American people learned about the dropping of the atomic bomb in Japan through a press release that was drafted long before the explosive was detonated. It read:

> *Statement by the President of the United States: Sixteen hours ago an American airplane dropped one bomb on—and destroyed its usefulness to the enemy. That bomb had more power than 20,000 tons [18,143 metric tons] of TNT ... The Japanese began the war from the air at Pearl Harbor. They have been repaid many fold. And the end is not yet. With this bomb we have now added a new and revolutionary increase in destruction to supplement the growing*

Opposite: President Truman spoke to the press about the atomic bombs, but only when he deemed it the right time to do so.

power of our armed forces. In their present form these bombs are now in production and even more powerful forms are in development.

It is an atomic bomb. It is a harnessing of the basic power of the universe. The force from which the sun draws its power has been loosed against those who brought war to the Far East.

The release continued to describe the massive, secretive, expensive research and development efforts that went into the creation of the bomb, and assured US citizens that the administration was not afraid to drop another bomb. It read, "We are now prepared to obliterate more rapidly and completely every productive enterprise the Japanese have above ground in any city. We shall destroy their docks, their factories, and their communications. Let there be no mistake; we shall completely destroy Japan's power to make war." The release asserted that the bomb was dropped in order to spare the Japanese people from "utter destruction." It spoke of a new era in war and in the possibility for energy production via atomic energy. Through the press release, the American people were told, in no uncertain terms, that their government was taking thoughtful actions in order to protect them and to end the war.

Reactions to the press release were mixed—pride, fear, disgust, joy. What the release didn't do was explain, in detail, just how many lives were snuffed out when the bomb was dropped. It didn't paint a picture of the total destruction of a city or, just days later, the destruction of another city when the second bomb was dropped. The release served to notify Americans that the United States had "won the race" to develop an atomic weapon, and that the government was taking every measure possible to end World War II.

Had the press release been 100 percent honest and forthcoming about the dropping of the atomic bomb, it would have described the hours-long flight in the *Enola Gay,* a B-29 bomber named after the mother of commander Paul Tibbets. On August 5, 1945, the plane was loaded on a secure air base on the island of Tinian. The crew members of the *Enola Gay* were not told about the bomb until the flight itself. The Manhattan Project had been so secretive that even those who were dropping the bomb had no idea, until it was about to happen, exactly what type of weapon they were carrying. The plane took off at 2:45 a.m. on August 6, accompanied by weather planes that made sure conditions were just right for the drop. Wind, storms, or other weather could disrupt plans and force the group to choose another city on which to drop the bomb. The team had initially wavered between the cities of Kyoto and Hiroshima—but Kyoto was ancient, holding great historical significance. Hiroshima, on the other hand, was an industrial city with ports and factories. With that, the fate of Hiroshima and its inhabitants was sealed. Fairly certain of its effectiveness, Oppenheimer and Groves had chosen the 5-ton (4.5-metric-ton) Little Boy, with its uranium core, to release above Hiroshima. At 8:15 a.m., on August 6, 1945, the bomb was dropped by parachute over the very center of Hiroshima.

When the bomb was just 1,903 feet (580 meters) over the city, the last of three detonators was activated, and the bomb exploded over the bridges, roads, factories, schools, homes, and everything else that made up the once-bustling urban area. Immediately, about eighty thousand people were killed

This photo of the atomic cloud over Hiroshima was taken from the *Enola Gay* after the dropping of the bomb.

from the blast, which produced extreme heat, vaporizing everything in its path. On the ground, there were fires, smoke, and a giant mushroom cloud that spread itself out over 2 miles (3.2 kilometers). This type of cloud is made up of debris, smoke, and condensed water vapor. Resembling a mushroom, it balloons out from the site of a nuclear explosion. The blast would end up decimating 4 square miles (10.4 square kilometers) of the city, leaving tens of thousands of people to die from wounds and radiation poisoning, a direct consequence of exposure to high amounts of radiation. The poisoning wreaks havoc on the body, causing violent nausea, vomiting, bleeding, hair loss, ulcers, the sloughing off of skin and, after hours or days, death.

While the mushroom cloud shot flames into the air, the *Enola Gay* and its accompanying planes zipped out of its reach. Colonel Paul W. Tibbets, the *Enola Gay*'s pilot, described the drop in an interview decades later, telling an interviewer:

As the bomb left the airplane, we took over manual control, made an extremely steep turn to try and put as much distance between ourselves and the explosion as possible. After we felt the explosion hit the airplane, that is the concussion waves, we knew that the bomb had exploded, and everything was a success. So we turned around to take a look at it. The site that greeted our eyes was quite beyond what we had expected, because we saw this cloud of boiling dust and debris below us with this tremendous mushroom on top. Beneath that was hidden the ruins of the city of Hiroshima.

Buildings were leveled. Firestorms and clouds of debris choked the streets. Pieces of hot iron and concrete flew in all directions. The blast was so hot it caused flesh to burn and internal organs to boil. Flying away as quickly as possible, the American crew was in shock: had they just won the war or made a terrible, unforgivable choice?

After the bombing, Hiroshima lay in tatters. Very little was salvageable.

All in all, about sixty thousand buildings were destroyed in the attack on Hiroshima. Final counts put the number of lives lost at 192,020, including the 80,000 individuals who perished in the initial blast. Three days after Hiroshima, the United States would drop another atomic bomb on Japan, this time on Nagasaki.

The Order to Drop the Bomb

The decision to drop the atomic bomb on Japan was not an easy one. It was not easy for Oppenheimer, who recoiled, disturbed, after watching the Trinity test. It was not easy for General Groves, who tensely waited to see if Japan would surrender before the drop. And it wasn't easy for President Truman, who had been brought into the atomic bomb conversation toward the end of the Manhattan Project and was tasked with resolving

British prime minister Clement Attlee (*seated left*), US president Harry Truman (*seated center*), and Russian premier Joseph Stalin (*seated right*) are pictured at the Potsdam Conference in 1945.

> ### And Furthermore
>
> In May 1945, the spring prior to the atomic bombings, President Truman authorized Secretary of War Henry Stimson to form the Interim Committee. This group of top officials was charged with developing a postwar atomic policy for the United States and recommending appropriate use of atomic weapons during World War II. This committee recommended that President Truman keep the bomb a secret until after it was dropped on Japan. It also concluded that the United States should attempt to remain the foremost nuclear power in the world, if possible.

a war that had been set in motion many years before he took over the office.

Throughout July 1945, President Truman was attending the Potsdam Conference in Germany. The meeting was held near Berlin from July 17 to August 2. In attendance at Potsdam were Premier Joseph Stalin of the Soviet Union, British prime minister Winston Churchill, and US president Harry S. Truman. The army chief of staff, George Marshall, was at Potsdam with President Truman, so George Handy was the acting chief of staff back in the United States.

The talks in Berlin centered around postwar Germany, but the conference attendees also issued a declaration that demanded unconditional surrender from Japan. This document, issued on July 26, listed the terms for Japanese surrender and threatened "prompt and utter destruction" if Japan chose not to surrender. What the Japanese did not know, but Stalin, Churchill, and Truman all knew, to varying degrees, was that the threatened destruction would result in the world's first-ever atomic bomb.

On July 25, 1945, the acting army chief of staff, Thomas Handy, wrote to Commanding General Carl Spaatz, ordering the US Air Force to "deliver its first special bomb as soon as weather will permit." The order went on to detail the planned drop as "after about 3 August 1945 on one of the targets: Hiroshima, Kokura, Nilgata and Nagasaki." It stated that military personnel and scientists would ride in additional planes in order to "observe and record the effects of the explosion of the bomb," suggested that additional bombs could and would be dropped on the aforementioned locations, and barred General Spaatz from sharing any information about the plans with anyone except the secretary of war and the president. This document was the official military order to drop the atomic bomb. Of course, ultimately nothing could be approved without the authorization of President Truman.

The very next day after the military order was issued, the Japanese rejected the Potsdam Declaration. They would not unconditionally surrender. The United States was aware, due to intercepted messages between Japan and Russia, that Japan was seeking a conditional surrender, which would leave its military dictatorship intact and potentially allow it to retain many of the lands it had gained during wartime. But the leaders from Potsdam would not relent. The war continued. July and August 1945 were bloody months on many sides. Both the United States and Japan suffered casualties as Japan continued to attack from underwater submarines and kamikaze aircraft. These planes were piloted by special members of the military who went on suicide missions, crashing their planes into American naval vessels with no chance for their survival. At the same time, US air raids over Japan using conventional bombs

Kamikaze planes, like the one in this illustration, were flown by pilots who intended to die for their country, often in violent plane crashes.

were happening daily, and innocent citizens were suffering starvation, illness, and death.

Seeking Alternatives

Surely there were alternatives to dropping an atomic weapon. More conventional bombing, ground battle, and increased naval activity were all options for a continued fight. However, the United States and its allies were interested in ending the war as quickly as possible, and they had threatened Japan with both quick and complete destruction if the country refused to unconditionally surrender. Many critics argue that a land invasion of Japan would have cost hundreds of thousands of lives, both American and Japanese, potentially causing more hurt than the eventual use of two atomic bombs. Even today, opinions remain varied and the topic continues to be a controversial one.

Persuading the President

On July 30, 1945, seven days before the drop, Henry Stimson, the secretary of war, wrote to President Truman, who was attending the Potsdam Conference. As director of the atomic bomb program, Stimson was instrumental in convincing Truman that the bomb should be put to use against the Japanese.

Stimson's message to Truman notified the president that "the time schedule on Groves' project is progressing so rapidly that it is now essential that a statement for release by you be available not later than Wednesday, 1 August." Stimson was requesting that Truman work with him to finalize the press release that would come out following the dropping of the bomb. Truman wrote a short, handwritten reply: "Sec War, Reply to your 41011 suggestions approved. Release when ready but not sooner than August 2. HST." With that exchange, the days began to tick down to the release of the bomb over Hiroshima. A statement was drafted. The bombs were readied on the island of Tinian.

Warning the Japanese

The dropping of the first atomic bomb was certainly a surprise to most people—American citizens, most American government workers, citizens of countries across the globe, and even some of the Allied leaders had no idea that the United States had produced a working bomb. The decision that sat on Truman's shoulders was a heavy one, especially since he was one of few people who knew about the deadly bombs and the toll they would take on Japan's citizens and land. Since the bombings, some critics have found fault with the lack of warning given to the Japanese. Truman, in letters to some of these critics, stated

Japan is a long, thin country with miles of coastline and many large cities.

that Japan's attack on Pearl Harbor also came as a great and terrible surprise.

Throughout World War II, it wasn't uncommon for bomber planes to drop leaflets before rounds of conventional bombing began. These would warn of coming explosions so that innocent citizens might take cover, while at the same time urging people to advocate for their government's surrender. A few days before the bombing of Hiroshima, millions of leaflets were dropped on Japanese cities, including Hiroshima and

Nagasaki. The papers, which would come to be known as the LeMay leaflets, did not directly speak to the atomic bomb. They read, in part, "in accordance with America's humanitarian policies, the American Air Force, which does not wish to injure innocent people, now gives you warning to evacuate the cities named and save your lives. America is not fighting the Japanese people but is fighting the military clique which has enslaved the Japanese people. The peace which America will bring will free people from the oppression of the military clique and mean the emergence of a new and better Japan." These words are, of course, translated from the original Japanese characters that were printed on the leaflets. It is hard to say if the fliers were any help to citizens living in Japanese cities, especially Hiroshima and, days later, Nagasaki.

Between the Bombs

If the decision to drop the world's first-ever atomic bomb was a difficult one, the choice to drop the second weapon was wrapped in even more pain, discomfort, and frustration. President Truman and his closest advisors were given to-the-minute updates about the bombing of Hiroshima and the subsequent lack of surrender on the part of Japan. The United States had developed an extremely technologically advanced, violent, deadly explosive before any other country was able to, and it was dropped on the enemy with a resounding blast. Tens of thousands of innocent people were killed instantly, and yet Japan did not surrender. The country's government and military stood, resolute in the face of a nuclear battle with which they could not equally compete, despite everything. Truman and the Allies were sure that the first bomb would convince Japan to give up. But it didn't.

The *Enola Gay* was a powerful, propeller-driven B-29 bomber. It can still be seen today, on display at exhibitions around the United States.

On August 7, 1945, just one day after the destruction in Hiroshima, Senator Richard Russell Jr. wrote to President Truman via telegram, urging him to take a hardline position on Japan, rather than act with mercy. His telegram read, in part, "Permit me to respectfully suggest that we cease our efforts to cajole Japan into surrendering in accordance with the Potsdam Declaration. Let us carry the war to them until they accept the unconditional surrender. The foul attack on Pearl Harbor brought us into war and I am unable to see any reason why we should be so much more considerate and lenient in dealing with Japan than with Germany." The telegram, which covered several pages, asserted that at least one more surprise bomb attack should visit Japan: "Our people have not forgotten that the Japanese struck us the first blow in this war without the slightest warning."

Senator Russell would get his wish. The Japanese War Council did not surrender after the bombing of Hiroshima, so the United States proceeded with plans to drop the next bomb.

From the start, multiple bombs were planned, though everyone hoped that only one would be needed. The second bombing was initially scheduled for August 11 but was moved up to August 9 due to poor weather reports.

Truman replied thoughtfully to Senator Russell on August 9, the day of the second atomic bombing. He wrote:

> *I read your telegram of August seventh with a lot of interest.*
>
> *I know that Japan is a terribly cruel and uncivilized nation in warfare but I can't bring myself to believe that, because they are beasts, we should ourselves set in the same manner.*
>
> *For myself, I certainly regret the necessity of wiping out whole populations because of the *pigheadedness* of the leaders of a nation and, for your information, I am not going to do it unless it is absolutely necessary. It is my opinion that after the Russians enter into war the Japanese will very shortly fold up.*
>
> *My object is to save as many American lives as possible but I also have a humane feeling for the women and children in Japan.*

President Truman was not enthusiastic about dropping the bombs. He fought internally and emotionally, weighing the options. Without another bomb, Japan might not surrender unconditionally, and even more Americans would surely have to give up their lives in bloody hand-to-hand combat. A second bomb could spell a quick and dirty end to a long and sorrowful war, but it wouldn't come without a major cost.

Another Bomb

The order on July 25 hadn't just authorized the use of one bomb. Item #2 was clearly written, "Additional bombs will be delivered on the above targets as soon as made ready by the project staff." Multiple cities were listed as targets. Truman was shaken by the first bombing and didn't necessarily want to continue, but the plans had been made. Without surrender from Japan, more atomic bombs would fall.

To take advantage of calm weather, the Fat Man bomb was rushed into readiness. Japan remained resolute—no unconditional surrender. The plane that would carry Fat Man was named *Bockscar*. It lifted off from the same island, Tinian, at 3:47 a.m. on August 9, 1945, and headed toward Japan. Its

This photo shows the remains of the Nagasaki Medical College after the atomic explosion in Nagasaki.

initial target was Kokura Arsenal, near the city of Kokura. The arsenal was a center for war industries, rather than a civilian hub. However, by the time the B-29 arrived, there was too much smoke and haze in the air to go through with the bombing over Kokura. As the plane was starting to run out of fuel and Japanese military were beginning to take notice, crewmen decided to head to the alternative target, Nagasaki, an industrial center and major port city.

Though Nagasaki was also obscured by a cloud, Captain Kermit K. Beahan dropped the bomb near the city's stadium. It exploded at 11:02 a.m. Nagasaki time. Most Americans were just falling asleep for the night, as Japan is fourteen hours ahead of the United States. Following the detonation, the mushroom cloud grew to over 60,000 feet (18,288 m) high. Over seventy thousand people were killed instantly in the blast. On the whole, it was comparable to the attack on Hiroshima just days before. Fire, death, and devastation.

On the evening of August 9 in the United States, President Truman was waiting to hear about the success of the second bomb drop, but he was also busy making a speech to the American people regarding the Potsdam Conference. In that speech, delivered over radio, Truman defended the bombing of Hiroshima and the use of the weapons:

> *I realize the tragic significance of the atomic bomb. Its production and its use were not lightly undertaken by this government. But we knew that our enemies were on the search for it. We know now how close they were to finding it. And we knew the disaster which would come to this nation, and to all peace-loving nations, to all civilization, if they*

> had found it first ... Having found the bomb we have used it. We have used it against those who attacked us without warning at Pearl Harbor, against those who have starved and beaten and executed American prisoners of war, against those who have abandoned all pretense of obeying international laws of warfare. We have used it in order to shorten the agony of war, in order to save the lives of thousands and thousands of young Americans. We shall continue to use it until we completely destroy Japan's power to make war. Only a Japanese surrender will stop us.

With that speech, President Truman not only noted the significance of the bomb, but he defended its creation and deployment, and set the stage for critics to assess the situation for years to come. For decades, researchers and historians have questioned just how close the Germans and Soviets were to creating their own atomic weapon. Of course, this

Japan's surrender took place aboard the USS *Missouri*. Here, General Yoshijiro Umeza signs the surrender document as General Douglas MacArthur (*across the desk*) and other soldiers look on.

> ### And Furthermore
>
> The Japanese military held two strong beliefs.: 1) loyalty to the emperor. 2) refusal to surrender. When the emperor himself stepped forward to surrender, everything was thrown into disarray. Some military members attempted a coup in order to continue the war. Others attempted to steal the emperor's recorded surrender speech so that it couldn't be broadcast. The minister of war was so torn between continuing the war and supporting the emperor that he committed suicide. For the Japanese, surrender was extremely difficult and unnatural, all the way until the bitter end.

quote tells us nothing about Truman's own internal struggle or guilt after the bombings. This message was crafted with a mind toward US citizens—what they wanted and needed to hear after their military caused hundreds of thousands of deaths over the course of just two quick morning bomb drops. The best defense of his decision, though, would come the next day, on August 10, 1945. Even as plans for additional atomic bomb drops continued in the United States, the Japanese held an imperial council, which ended in a 3–3 tied vote on surrender. In an unprecedented move, the Japanese emperor, Emperor Hirohito, came forward to break the tie, ordering his country to surrender to the Allies. It was nearly unconditional in nature. In the end, Japan insisted that the emperor be allowed to remain the head of state in name only, with no true power. The Allies agreed to the terms. To supporters, the results were clear. The dropping of the atomic bombs had worked. World War II was finally put to rest.

Religious Opposition

Almost immediately following the bombing, Reverend Dr. Samuel Cavert wrote to President Truman to report concern and discontent within the Christian community about the dropping of the

Reverend Dr. Samuel Cavert (*right*) in December 1950

nuclear bomb. Cavert was a well-regarded ecumenical leader and one of the chief architects of the National Council of Churches and the World Council of Churches. On August 9, 1945, he sent a telegram to Truman. It read: "Many Christians deeply disturbed over use of atomic bombs against Japanese cities because of their necessarily indiscriminate destructive efforts and because their use sets an extremely dangerous precedent for future of mankind." He went on to warn the president that leaders from the National Council were preparing a statement urging that the United States give Japan the opportunity to reconsider the ultimatum before dropping more bombs. However, that very day, the Fat Man bomb would be dropped on Nagasaki. President Truman sent a telegram back to Cavert on August 11. He wrote, "Nobody is more disturbed over the use of Atomic bombs than I am but I was greatly disturbed over the unwarranted attack by the Japanese on Pearl Harbor and their murder of our prisoners of war. The only language they seem to understand is the one we have been using to bombard them. When you have to deal with a beast you have to treat him as a beast. It is most regrettable but nevertheless true."

Chapter Three

Leaving a Legacy

The close of World War II wasn't the end of the story of the atomic bomb. In fact, it was just the beginning. What started as intriguing scientific discoveries in Europe had crossed the Atlantic and grown into something very real and dangerous. The fears these dangers ignited in the hearts and minds of Americans, coupled with the $2 billion price tag of the Manhattan Project, turned into plans for two deadly weapons. Those plans, of course, then transformed into real bombs with the power to destroy tens of thousands of people in seconds. With the order to drop the atomic bomb (and any necessary, subsequent bombs) authorized by President Truman, those weapons created devastation for the people of both Hiroshima and Nagasaki, Japan, as well as for all those within the country

Opposite: In 2016, activists of all ages came together in Washington, DC, to protest the stockpiling and use of nuclear weapons.

who mourned the dead and struggled to come to terms with surrender. The order also helped to create a suspended, temporary state of peace that the world hadn't known for many years, and a feeling amongst Americans that the war had been won through atomic weaponry. To the Japanese, though, a major crime had been committed for which there was little to no justification. Elsewhere across the globe, other countries felt compelled to begin their own nuclear programs, establishing arsenals and beginning a state of cold war that would continue for decades into the future.

Short-Term Effects and Reactions

Most of the short-term effects of the bombs are clear—destruction of cities, Japan's surrender in the days following the attacks—but then, days, months, and even years after the bombs, civilians from Hiroshima and Nagasaki began to show signs of advanced radiation sickness. Their hair and teeth fell out, sores tore into their flesh, and pregnant women suffered miscarriages. Babies were born with extreme deformities. While some lived with the disease, many others died. In Japan, the survivors are called *hibakusha*, or "explosion-affected people." Over one hundred thousand of these people are still alive today, and they are still telling their stories. From the Japanese government, the *hibakusha* receive financial and medical support. From the United States, they receive nothing.

In the years immediately following the bombs, the Allies actually censored the Japanese press from reporting on the aftermath of the bombings and forbade victims from telling

The atomic bombings didn't just cause loss of life. They also left people disfigured, sick, and affected for the rest of their lives. This survivor displays her deformed hands twenty years after the bombing.

their stories. Today, many programs and nonprofit organizations are in place to help people across the world understand the history of the atomic bomb, its use, and what we can learn from what happened.

Though the United States did have a small arsenal of nuclear bombs it planned to use if Japan had not surrendered, Nagasaki became the last target of World War II. Immediately following the end of the war, the American military occupied Japan, led by General Douglas MacArthur. Military trials, also

> **And Furthermore**
>
> Atomic energy can be harnessed to generate electricity. As of 2016, there were over four hundred nuclear reactors producing electricity in thirty countries around the world. Nuclear reactors generate heat, which then powers a steam turbine. These plants are considered relatively safe.

known as tribunals, were held for Japanese and Nazi military leaders, and many of them were put to death by hanging. This action, violent though it was, left some with a sense of justice and also helped to prevent dictatorial—all-powerful—leadership from taking control in these countries again. For many Americans, the United States is the hero of the atomic age. It was the first country to develop and use an atomic weapon, and its use effectively brought an end to World War II. Many argue that deaths would have occurred at a furious rate had the United States gone into ground combat in Japan, even with the potential aid of the Soviet Union. For some, the bomb was the only way.

For people around the world, the sudden use of the atomic bomb was shocking at best. What had once been a closely guarded secret of the American military was suddenly put into stark, public focus. US military officials, in an effort to keep ahold of many of the secrets, carefully controlled the dissemination of information around the nuclear program. They drafted press releases to follow both bombs, which shared selective information about the Trinity test, research, and development behind the bombs. The releases also spoke to the possibility of using nuclear technology to produce electricity. For the time being, military security was somewhat secured,

Joseph Stalin gives a speech in 1945. Like others, he didn't understand the true power of the atomic bomb until the day it was dropped.

and US citizens held a favorable view of the atomic bomb. After the war, nearly everyone regarded the atomic bomb as the war-ender that had saved countless American lives. Very few were sympathetic toward Japan, especially after nearly four relentless years of war.

Long-Term Effects

Opinions about a charged topic like atomic bombs certainly wouldn't remain static. The world's collective understanding of war, death, justice, and the like were forever changed by the introduction of atomic weapons. Globally, the tide first turned toward weapons, and it has only escalated since. More and more countries began to build and acquire their own nuclear bombs.

Today, about thirty countries have nuclear power plants, but only nine possess nuclear weapons: Russia, the United States, China, India, Israel, France, North Korea, Pakistan, and the United Kingdom. A global security foundation called the Ploughshares Fund reports there are more than fifteen

In the 1950s, many families invested in underground bomb shelters in an attempt to protect themselves against future attacks.

thousand nuclear weapons around the world today. The countries with the most? Russia and the United States.

During World War II, the United States strategically kept information about the Manhattan Project secret from Stalin and other Soviet Union leaders. Truman and his advisors didn't want the Soviet Union to gain a foothold in the realm of atomic technology.

> ### And Furthermore
>
> Though wounds remain, reconciliation progress was made when the US Ambassador to Japan visited the Peace Memorial in 2004. Today, it's tradition for US ambassadors to visit the memorial. In 2016, President Obama visited the Peace Memorial, while Prime Minister Shinzo Abe visited Pearl Harbor.

For Truman, this plan backfired. Following the war, amidst attempts to redistribute and rebuild countries across the globe, divisions between Western democracies and Communist ideologies began to deepen. The Soviet Union and the United States began to arm themselves with more technologically advanced weapons. From the first nuclear bombs were born thermonuclear hydrogen bombs, and then missiles that could carry bombs directly across the ocean to targets on other continents. The stockpiling of these weapons acted as a deterrent when the other made unfavorable political actions. This period, known officially as the Cold War, continued from 1945 into the early 1990s. The war was considered "cold" because no fighting actually took place, though there were extremely tense periods and many, many threats of violence. In the 1990s, the Soviet Union dissolved. Both the United States and Russia then agreed to a series of treaties that shrunk both countries' arsenals, though they still possess far more nuclear weapons than any other country in the world.

Today, the United Nations encourages most countries to refrain from beginning or continuing nuclear programs that are not solely intended to produce electricity. When countries do take steps toward nuclear armament, other nations often put sanctions in place that bar the offending country from receiving necessary imports like food and oil. Working together across the entire planet, the global community has kept nuclear armaments in check—for the most part. The United States and Russia continue to hold huge numbers of these deadly weapons. There are many organizations dedicated to the destruction of all nuclear bombs, no matter which country possesses them. Many believe that getting rid of atomic bombs is the only way to achieve true peace and unity in the long term. With nuclear

Today, nuclear missiles are smaller, faster, and more powerful than ever before.

Nuclear Threats Today

In 2018, we did not find ourselves far from the tense days of the Cold War, or even World War II, though communication styles have transitioned from telegrams to social media messages. North Korean dictator Kim Jong Un and US president Donald Trump exchanged terse threats over Twitter during the first part of the year. While the United States has been in possession of many powerful nuclear weapons since the 1940s, North Korea has slowly built its arsenal over the last couple decades, and has now been conducting nuclear bomb tests and military exercises in order to show its strength. To retaliate, Trump began referring to Kim Jong Un as "Rocket Man" in his tweets and boasted of his "nuclear button" that was "much bigger" than North Korea's.

weapons still in play, all we might have is mutually assured destruction (MAD), or the knowledge that we hold the power to destroy ourselves, all of us.

Most of the global nuclear tests were completed in the thirty years following the creation of the first bomb. The Soviet Union, having planted spies in the Manhattan Project since its very inception, ran its first open nuclear test in 1949. The 1950s and 1960s saw Great Britain, France, China, and India acquire nuclear weapons technology. The spread of nuclear

North Korean leader Kim Jong Un stands with his generals at a defense detachment in May 2017.

weapons technology is known as nuclear proliferation. Pakistan conducted its first test in 1998 and North Korea began tests in 2006. Today, as in 1945, some of the most threatening countries are those run by powerful dictators. The United States and the United Nations have tried for years to dissuade North Korea from adopting nuclear technology and pushed them hard to get rid of their bombs. North Korea, however, is not budging. Kim Jong Un, the country's leader, is set on having nuclear weapons—and on making sure everyone knows it. Of course, the world's biggest nuclear powers, Russia and the United States, aren't about to give up their nuclear weapons either. With the decision to drop the atomic bomb, and even before that authorization, in the years of research, development, and consideration that went into its eventual deployment, the atomic age was set in motion. The world was forever changed, for better or for worse—we may not yet know for sure.

Glossary

Allied powers A group of united countries during World War II that included Great Britain, the United States, China, and the Soviet Union.

atom An extremely small unit of matter; it defines the structure of an element.

Axis powers A group of countries that fought against the Allies in World War II, led by Germany, Italy, and Japan.

chain reaction A series of changes or reactions in which each one initiates the next.

Cold War A state of hostilities from around 1950 to 1990. It is marked by a lack of open warfare in favor of threats, propaganda, and other posturing.

conditional surrender A surrender in which one side will only give up if certain criteria are met.

dictatorial The characteristics of a ruler with total power.

element One of over one hundred substances that cannot be broken down into a simpler substance. Each element is identified by the number of protons inside the atom's nucleus.

emperor Historically, the highest-ranking leader in Japan.

Fat Man An implosion bomb that was dropped over Nagasaki, Japan.

hibakusha The Japanese word for those who survived the atomic bombings of 1945.

implosion The action of something collapsing inward rather than outward.

Interim Committee A secret group, created in 1945 and authorized by President Truman, that advised on all matters relating to nuclear energy.

kamikaze Japanese aircraft carrying pilots on suicide missions that purposefully crashed planes into enemy targets.

Little Boy The first nuclear weapon used in war, this bomb had a gun-like design.

Manhattan Project The secret program used to develop atomic weapons in the United States during World War II.

mushroom cloud A mushroom-shaped cloud that forms after a nuclear explosion.

Nazi A member of the National Socialist German Workers' Party.

Glossary • 55

nuclear fission The moment when a nucleus splits, creating energy.

nuclear proliferation The spread of nuclear weapons across the globe, especially to countries that do not already possess them.

Potsdam Conference A meeting between the Allied leaders held in late summer 1945.

radiation poisoning A damaging sickness caused by exposure to radiation.

radioactivity The spontaneous emission of energetic particles by some atoms.

reconciliation The return of friendly relations after an argument, disagreement, or conflict.

theater In wartime, an area of land, sea, or air in which important military operations are occurring.

ultimatum A final demand or condition that, if not met, will result in force or other action.

Further Information

Books

Adams, Simon. *DK Eyewitness Books: World War II.* London, UK: DK Publishing, 2014.

Coerr, Eleanor. *Sadako and the Thousand Paper Cranes.* New York: G.P. Putnam's Sons, 1977.

Fetter-Vorm, Jonathan. *Trinity: A Graphic History of the First Atomic Bomb.* New York: Hill and Wang, 2012.

Lawton, Clive A. *Hiroshima: The Story of the First Atom Bomb.* Cambridge, MA: Candlewick Press, 2004.

Yep, Laurence. *Hiroshima.* New York: Scholastic, 1997.

Websites

BBC Bitesize: The Bombing of Hiroshima

https://www.bbc.co.uk/education/guides/z8y82hv/revision

Here you can read about the historic dropping of the first atomic bomb, do activities, and test your knowledge with a quiz.

The Enola Gay

http://www.enolagay509th.com

Including photos, timelines, stories, articles, technical information, and more, this site is the official web page of Paul W. Tibbets, who piloted the *Enola Gay*.

Exploratorium: Remembering Nagasaki

http://www.exploratorium.edu/nagasaki/index.html

Built for the fiftieth anniversary of the bombings, this site includes photos by a Japanese army photographer and a public forum about the atomic age.

Voice of Hibakusha

https://www.inicom.com/hibakusha

In Japan, the word *hibakusha* refers to those affected by the atomic bombings. This site offers firsthand accounts from survivors.

Bibliography

Atomic Heritage Foundation. "Little Boy and Fat Man." July 23, 2014. https://www.atomicheritage.org/history/little-boy-and-fat-man.

———. "Warning Leaflets." 2017. https://www.atomicheritage.org/key-documents/warning-leaflets.

Bankston, John. *Edward Teller and the Development of the Hydrogen Bomb*. Bear, DE: Mitchell Lane Publishers, 2002.

Chuck, Elizabeth. "Fact Sheet: Who Has Nuclear Weapons, and How Many Do They Have?" NBC News. March 31, 2016. https://www.nbcnews.com/news/world/fact-sheet-who-has-nuclear-weapons-how-many-do-they-n548481.

Crewe, Sabrina. *The Atom Bomb Project*. Events That Shaped America. New York: Gareth Stevens Publishing, 2005.

Engdahl, Sylvia, ed. *The Atomic Bombings of Hiroshima and Nagasaki*. New York: Greenhaven Publishing, 2011.

Fetter-Vorm, Jonathan. *Trinity: A Graphic History of the First Atomic Bomb*. New York: Hill and Wang, 2012.

Gonzales, Doreen. *The Manhattan Project and the Atomic Bomb in American History.* New York: Enslow Publishers, 2000.

Hall, Michelle. "By the Numbers: World War II's Atomic Bombs." CNN Library. August 6, 2013. http://www.cnn.com/2013/08/06/world/asia/btn-atomic-bombs/index.html.

Harry S. Truman Presidential Library and Museum. "The Decision to Drop the Atomic Bomb: Documents." 2017. https://www.trumanlibrary.org/whistlestop/study_collections/bomb/large/index.php?action=docs.

Lawton, Clive A. *Hiroshima: The Story of the First Atom Bomb.* Cambridge, MA: Candlewick Press, 2004.

Miscamble, Wilson D. *The Most Controversial Decision: Truman, the Atomic Bombs, and the Defeat of Japan.* New York: Cambridge, 2011.

National Park Service. "Harry S. Truman's Decision to Use the Atomic Bomb." https://www.nps.gov/articles/trumanatomicbomb.htm.

Poolos, Jamie. *The Atomic Bombings of Hiroshima and Nagasaki.* New York: Infobase Publishing, 2008.

Siegel, Robert, and Melissa Block. "Pilot of Enola Gay Had No Regrets for Hiroshima." NPR. November 1, 2007. https://www.npr.org/templates/story/story.php?storyId=15858203.

Sonneborn, Liz. *The Manhattan Project.* New York: Chelsea House, 2011.

Sullivan, Edward T. *The Ultimate Weapon: The Race to Develop the Atomic Bomb.* New York: Holiday House, 2007.

Tohmatsu, Haruo. "The 'Gettysburg in the Pacific' and Japan-U.S. Reconciliation." *Japan Times.* March 2, 2017. https://www.japantimes.co.jp/opinion/2017/03/02/commentary/japan-commentary/gettysburg-pacific-japan-u-s-reconciliation/#.Wk8LfxNSxE5.

Tracy, Kathleen. *Top Secret: The Story of the Manhattan Project.* Hockessin, DE: Mitchell Lane Publishers, 2006.

US Department of Energy Office of History and Heritage Resources. "The Manhattan Project: An Interactive History. Dawn of the Atomic Era (1945)." https://www.osti.gov/opennet/manhattan-project-history/Events/1945/1945.htm.

Index

Page numbers in **boldface** are illustrations.

Allied powers, 8, 21, 34, 40, 44
alternatives, 31, 38
atom, 8–10, **9**, 15
atomic age, 46, 53
Axis powers, 6, 8

blockade, 19
Bockscar, 37

Cavert, Samuel, 41, **41**
chain reaction, 10–11, 15
Cold War, 5, 44, 49, 51
conditional surrender, 30
conventional bombs, 5, 16, 30–31, 33
coup, 40
Curie, Marie, 8

defense, 38–40
dictatorial, 46
domino effect, 10

Einstein, Albert, 11, **12**
element, 8–10, 12
emperor, 40
energy production, 24, 46

Enola Gay, 25–26, **35**

Fat Man, 15–16, **16**, 37, 41

ground combat, 31, 46
Groves, Leslie, 13–14, 19, 21, 25, 28, 32

hibakusha, 44
Hiroshima, 25, 27–28, **28**, 30, 32–35, 38, 43–44
Hitler, Adolf, 6, **7**, 11, 19

implosion, 15, 17
Interim Committee, 29
internment camps, 19

kamikaze, 30, **31**
Kim Jong Un, 51, **52**, 53

LeMay leaflets, 34
Little Boy, **4**, 15, **16**, 17, 25
Los Alamos, 14–15, **14**

Manhattan Project, 13, 15, 18, 25, 28, 43, 49, 51
mushroom cloud, 26–27, **26**, 38

mutually assured destruction (MAD), 51

Nagasaki, 28, 30, 34, **37**, 38, 41, 43–45
Nazi, 6, 11, 46
North Korea, 48, 51–53
nuclear fission, 10, 13
nuclear power plants, 10, 48
nuclear proliferation, 52

Oppenheimer, J. Robert, 14–16, 20–21, 25, 28

Pearl Harbor, 7–8, 13, 19, 23, 33, 35, 39, 41, 49
plutonium, 8, 15
Potsdam Conference, 21, **28**, 29, 32, 38
Potsdam Declaration, 20, 30, 35
press release, 17, 21, 23–25, 32, 46

race, 15, 21, 24
radiation poisoning, 26, 44
radioactivity, 8
reconciliation, 49
Roosevelt, Franklin Delano, 6, 11, 13, 18–19

Russell, Richard, Jr., 35–36

secretive, 13–15, 17–18, 24–25, 29, 46, 49
social media, 51
spies, 19, 51
Stalin, Joseph, **28**, 29, **47**, 49
Stimson, Henry Lewis, 21, **21**, 29, 32
Szilard, Leo, 10–11

telegram, 21, 35–36, 41, 51
theater, 19
thermonuclear hydrogen bombs, 49
Tibbets, Paul, 25–27
Tinian, 20, 25, 32, 37
tribunal, 46
Trinity test, 16–17, **17**, 19, 28, 46
Truman, Harry S., 18–19, 21, **22**, 28–30, **28**, 32, 34–41, 43, 49

ultimatum, 41
unconditional surrender, 29, 35–37, 40
uranium, 8, 10–11, 15, 25

Index • 63

About the Author

Kaitlyn Duling believes in the power of words to change hearts, minds, and, ultimately, actions. An author, poet, and grant writer who grew up in Illinois, she now resides in Pittsburgh, Pennsylvania. She knows that knowledge of the past is the key to our future and wants to make sure that all children and families have access to high-quality information.